HAMMOND
the animal atlas

Anita Ganeri

Mapmakers for the 21st Century

Published in the United States, Canada, and Puerto Rico
by Hammond World Atlas Corporation
Springfield, New Jersey 07081
www.hammondmap.com

Copyright © 2006 Orpheus Books Ltd.

Created and produced by Rachel Coombs, Nicholas Harris,
Sarah Harrison, Sarah Hartley and Emma Helbrough,
Orpheus Books Ltd.

Text Anita Ganeri

Illustrated by Susanna Addario, Graham Austin, Andrew Beckett,
John Butler, Martin Camm, Ferruccio Cucchiarini, Peter Dennis,
Malcolm Ellis, Betti Ferrero, Giuliano Fornari, Ray Grinaway,
Gary Hincks, Inklink, Ian Jackson, John Morris, Steve Noon, Eric Robson,
Nicki Palin, Claudia Saraceni, Ivan Stalio, Colin Woolf, David Wright

ISBN 0-8437-0918-9

Printed and bound in China

CONTENTS

THE WORLD

FROM THE icy Poles to the baking deserts, animals live all over the world. They are specially adapted to survive in their habitats, their natural homes.

Tropical rain forests grow near the Equator, where it is warm and humid all year round. They are home to at least half of all the world's plant and animal species.

Rain forest

At either end of the Earth lie the polar regions— the Arctic in the north and the continent of Antarctica in the south. Freezing temperatures, icy winds, and long, dark winters make these very hostile habitats for all but a few animals.

Polar

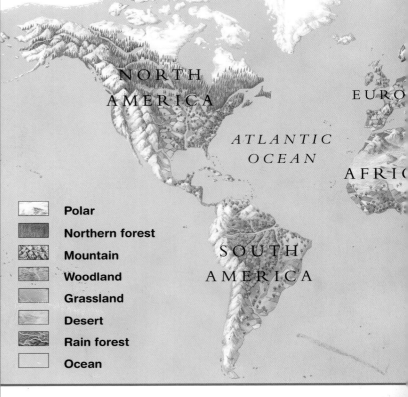

NORTH AMERICA

ATLANTIC OCEAN

EURO

AFRIC

SOUTH AMERICA

- Polar
- Northern forest
- Mountain
- Woodland
- Grassland
- Desert
- Rain forest
- Ocean

Mountains are found in all the world's continents, both in warm and cold regions. The higher up you are, the colder the temperatures. There are many mountain habitats, ranging from the forests of the lower foothills to the grassy meadows or rocky ground higher up the slopes. The peaks of some mountains are covered in ice and snow all year round. The animals that live in these habitats must cope with the bitter cold of a mountain winter.

Mountain

Grasslands are vast open plains. They cover more than a quarter of the Earth's surface. They occur in places that are too dry for many trees to grow, but which receive enough rain for grasses to grow. They provide food for herds of grazing animals, such as antelope, zebra, and wildebeest. These, in turn, attract predators, such as lions.

Woodlands are mostly found to the south of the northern forests, where the climate is milder and wetter.

Woodland

Northern forest

A wide band of forest stretches across the northern regions of North America, Europe, and Asia. The trees are mostly conifers, such as pine, spruce, and fir. They provide food and shelter for the animals that live there.

Temperate woodland is made up of broadleaved and deciduous trees, such as oak, maple, and beech. In winter, the woods may seem bare and lifeless. In summer, they are rich in wildlife—deer, foxes, and birds.

ARCTIC OCEAN

ASIA

PACIFIC OCEAN

INDIAN OCEAN

AUSTRALASIA

Desert

Deserts may be sandy, rocky, or pebbly. They are some of the driest places on Earth. Only the hardiest animals can survive. Desert animals have developed various ways of coping with the conditions. Many can go for long periods without water. Some get all the water they need from their food. To avoid the baking hot desert day, many animals are nocturnal. They hunt for food at night when it is cooler.

Grassland

More than two-thirds of the Earth's surface is covered by the oceans. The richest variety of ocean wildlife is found close to coral reefs in warm, shallow seas. These beautiful underwater gardens teem with fish, sponges, and numerous shellfish.

Ocean

THE WORLD

NORTH AMERICA

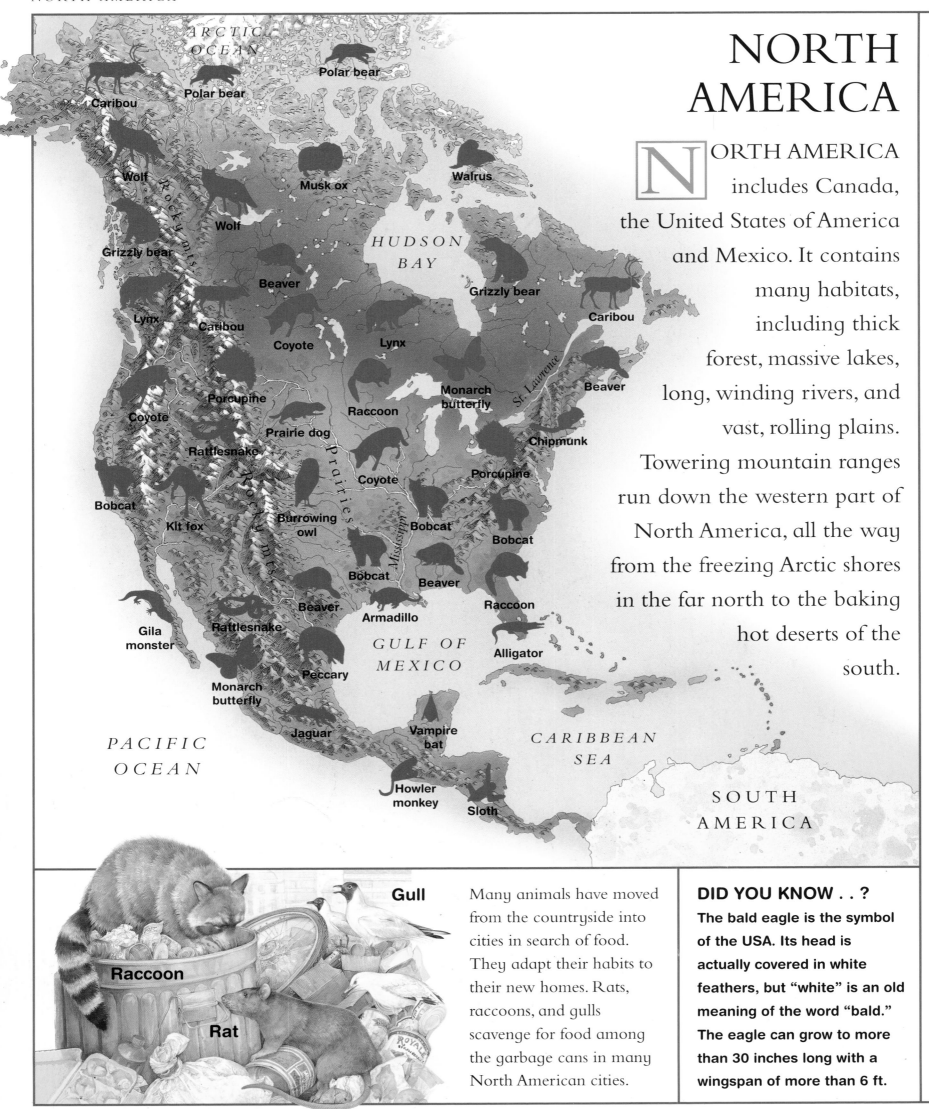

ARCTIC OCEAN

Polar bear

Polar bear

Caribou

Walrus

Wolf

Musk ox

Wolf

Grizzly bear

HUDSON BAY

Beaver

Grizzly bear

Caribou

Lynx

Caribou

Lynx

Coyote

Beaver

Monarch butterfly

St. Lawrence

Porcupine

Raccoon

Chipmunk

Coyote

Prairie dog

Porcupine

Rattlesnake

Coyote

Bobcat

Bobcat

Burrowing owl

Bobcat

Kit fox

Mississippi

Beaver

Bobcat

Beaver

Gila monster

Rattlesnake

Armadillo

Raccoon

GULF OF MEXICO

Alligator

Peccary

Monarch butterfly

Jaguar

Vampire bat

CARIBBEAN SEA

PACIFIC OCEAN

Howler monkey

Sloth

SOUTH AMERICA

N ORTH AMERICA includes Canada, the United States of America and Mexico. It contains many habitats, including thick forest, massive lakes, long, winding rivers, and vast, rolling plains. Towering mountain ranges run down the western part of North America, all the way from the freezing Arctic shores in the far north to the baking hot deserts of the south.

Gull

Raccoon

Rat

Many animals have moved from the countryside into cities in search of food. They adapt their habits to their new homes. Rats, raccoons, and gulls scavenge for food among the garbage cans in many North American cities.

DID YOU KNOW . . ?
The bald eagle is the symbol of the USA. Its head is actually covered in white feathers, but "white" is an old meaning of the word "bald." The eagle can grow to more than 30 inches long with a wingspan of more than 6 ft.

In the North American Midwest lie grassland plains known as the prairies. They once covered a huge area but now are mostly given over to farmland. Prairie dogs are rodents that dig large networks of burrows, tunnels, and chambers under the ground. Long ago, a prairie dog "town" may have been home to millions of prairie dogs.

The Everglades in Florida is a large area of swampy marshland. It is a precious haven for many species, including wading birds and the American alligator.

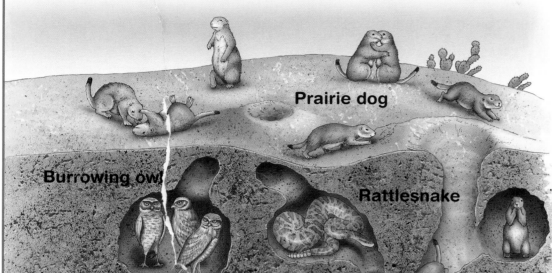

Large parts of southwestern USA and northern Mexico are rocky deserts. By day, temperatures can soar to 110°F, but, by night, they can fall to below freezing. Many desert animals, such as the kit fox, rest during the day and come out at night to hunt for food. The kit fox uses its large ears and superb hearing to track down its prey of lizards and other small animals. It chases after its victim before pouncing.

NORTH AMERICA

Chipmunk

The chipmunk is a type of rodent. It lives in North American woods and forests. In summer, it collects nuts, seeds, and berries in its cheeks. It stores the food underground, ready for winter when it hibernates.

Porcupine

Porcupines are found in forests right across North America. They feed on conifer needles, bark, leaves, buds, roots, and berries. A porcupine uses its needle-sharp quills to defend itself. It spreads out its quills, turns around, and lashes out at its attacker with its prickly tail.

Beaver

Beavers are superbly adapted to life around North American lakes and creeks. Their back feet are webbed for swimming and their coats are sleek and waterproof. A beaver uses its large tail as a rudder for steering as it swims. If danger threatens, it slaps the water with its tail as it dives. Underwater, it can hold its breath for up to 15 minutes. Beavers are also brilliant builders. With their strong teeth, they gnaw through tree trunks which they use to build a dam across a creek. In the pond that forms behind the dam, they construct a lodge out of mud and sticks.

Monarch butterfly

Every year, in September, millions of monarch butterflies begin an amazing journey. These insects fly nearly 2000 miles from Canada to California and Mexico. Here, millions of monarchs gather in thick clusters on forest trees where they spend the winter *(below)*. As spring approaches, they leave their roosts to feed and find a mate before they begin their journey back north again in February or March.

Monarch butterfly caterpillars have striking black, yellow, and white stripes. This bright coloring warns hungry predators that they are poisonous. Monarch caterpillars feed on a plant called milkweed. This contains a poison that stays inside their bodies. As they eat and grow, the caterpillars shed their skins *(above)*.

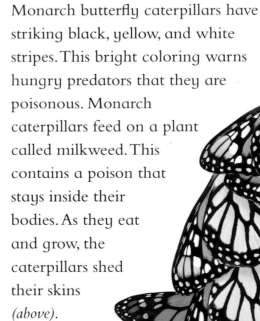

The huge grizzly bear stands up to 10 feet tall and may weigh almost half a ton. It is named for its grizzled (gray-tipped) fur. Grizzlies are immensely strong and can kill an animal as big as a caribou with their front claws. They also eat fish, rodents, and berries. Large numbers of grizzlies have been wiped out by hunting and loss of habitat. Today, they are rare.

Grizzly bear

In the northern forests, gray wolves live and hunt in packs. They howl to keep in touch with each other and to warn rival packs away. The wolves set out in single file to track their prey of musk oxen or moose. Once the prey is sighted, the wolves stand still. As soon as the animal starts to run, the wolves suddenly rush forward into the attack. For protection, musk oxen form a tight circle around their young. They use their sharp horns as weapons for self-defense.

Musk oxen

Gray wolf

Bobcat

The bobcat lives on rocky or forested mountain slopes. Its spotted coat blends in well with its background, allowing it to creep up on its prey unseen. Bobcats feed mainly on rabbits and birds. They sometimes hunt porcupines, flipping them over to avoid their deadly quills *(see opposite)*.

Caribou live in herds, thousands of animals strong. Every winter, the herds migrate from their summer breeding grounds in the far north of Canada to the forests farther south.

Caribou

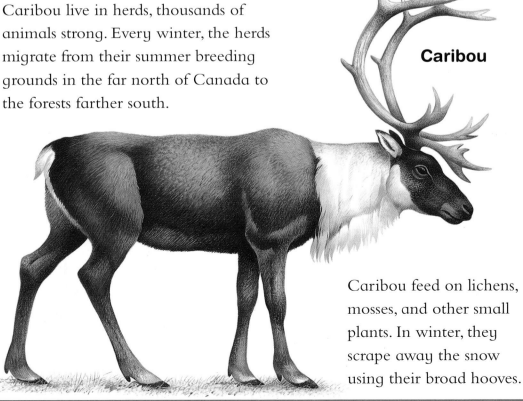

Caribou feed on lichens, mosses, and other small plants. In winter, they scrape away the snow using their broad hooves.

FOREST AND TUNDRA

SOUTH AMERICA

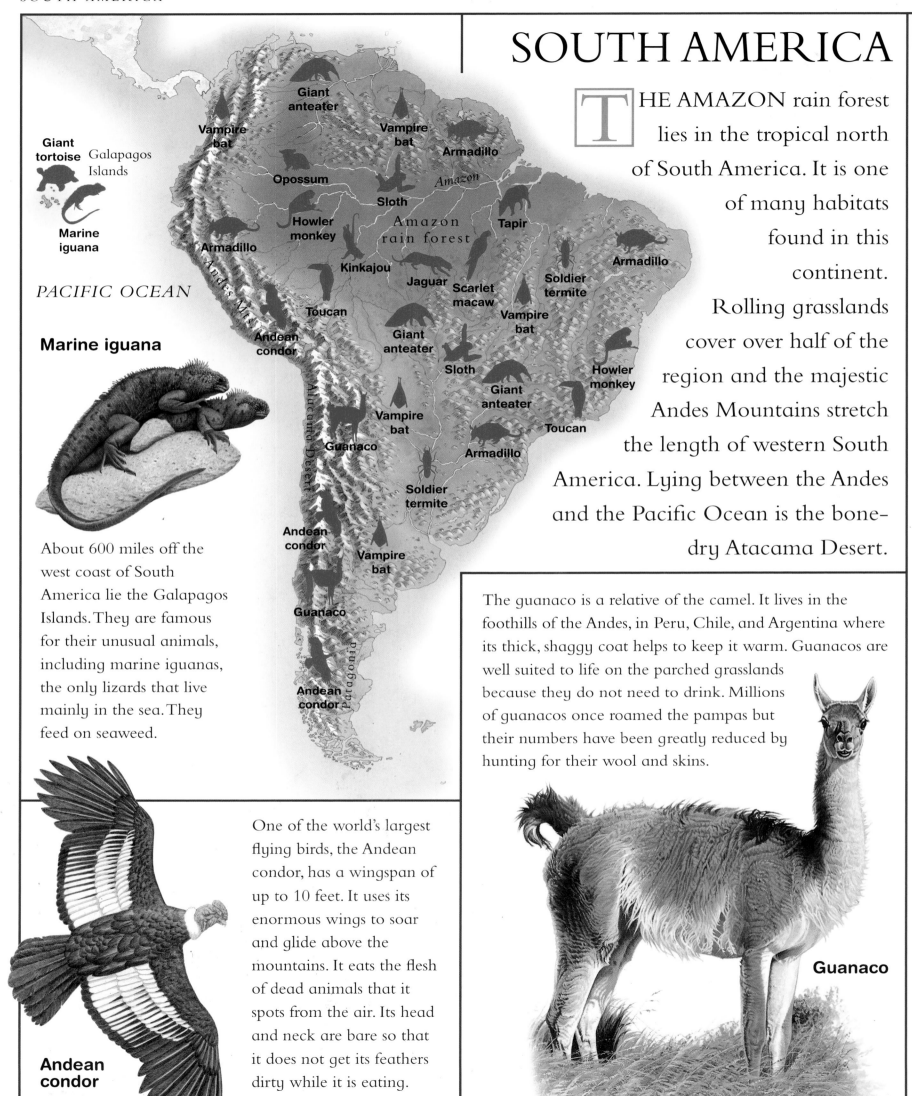

THE AMAZON rain forest lies in the tropical north of South America. It is one of many habitats found in this continent. Rolling grasslands cover over half of the region and the majestic Andes Mountains stretch the length of western South America. Lying between the Andes and the Pacific Ocean is the bone-dry Atacama Desert.

Marine iguana

About 600 miles off the west coast of South America lie the Galapagos Islands. They are famous for their unusual animals, including marine iguanas, the only lizards that live mainly in the sea. They feed on seaweed.

Andean condor

One of the world's largest flying birds, the Andean condor, has a wingspan of up to 10 feet. It uses its enormous wings to soar and glide above the mountains. It eats the flesh of dead animals that it spots from the air. Its head and neck are bare so that it does not get its feathers dirty while it is eating.

The guanaco is a relative of the camel. It lives in the foothills of the Andes, in Peru, Chile, and Argentina where its thick, shaggy coat helps to keep it warm. Guanacos are well suited to life on the parched grasslands because they do not need to drink. Millions of guanacos once roamed the pampas but their numbers have been greatly reduced by hunting for their wool and skins.

Guanaco

Map labels: Giant tortoise, Galapagos Islands, Marine iguana, PACIFIC OCEAN, Giant anteater, Vampire bat, Vampire bat, Armadillo, Opossum, Amazon, Sloth, Howler monkey, Amazon rain forest, Tapir, Armadillo, Kinkajou, Jaguar, Scarlet macaw, Soldier termite, Toucan, Andean condor, Giant anteater, Vampire bat, Armadillo, Sloth, Howler monkey, Giant anteater, Vampire bat, Guanaco, Toucan, Armadillo, Soldier termite, Andean condor, Vampire bat, Guanaco, Patagonia, Andean condor, Andes Mts, Atacama Desert

Vampire bat

The vampire bat preys on large animals, such as cattle, horses and hogs. It attacks its victims at night. The bat nips an animal's skin with its razor-sharp teeth, then laps up the blood that oozes out of the wound. Its spit contains chemicals that stop the blood from clotting so it flows freely. Vampires do not take enough blood to kill their prey but they can spread diseases, such as rabies.

Nine-banded armadillo

The nine-banded armadillo protects itself from its enemies with a coat of tough armor. Its armor is made from strong, bony plates, covered in horny scales. Armadillos use the sharp claws on their front feet for digging tunnels. They spend most of their time underground.

Several different species of giant tortoise live on the Galapagos Islands. Each has a slightly differently shaped shell. These huge reptiles can grow up to 5 feet long and weigh more than 400 pounds. They may live for 200 years, longer than any other animal. They feed on almost any type of green plants.

Giant tortoise

DID YOU KNOW . . ?
Animals that live high up in the Andes Mountains have to cope with very thin air. Some have larger hearts and lungs than usual to allow them to make best use of the little oxygen available.

Soldier termite

Termites are small insects. They live in colonies up to 10 million strong. Master builders, they construct tall mud towers, or mounds, that contain chambers, including living quarters and food "gardens."

The amazing giant anteater lives on the grassy plains of South America known as the pampas. It feeds on ants and termites, and must eat more than 20,000 of them a day in order to survive. It uses smell to locate a termite mound or ants' nest, then breaks it open with its sharp claws. Then it flicks its long, sticky tongue in and out of the nest to lap up the ants or termites. Finding enough to eat is hard work—the anteater may have to visit 30 nests an hour to fill itself up.

Giant anteater

MOUNTAIN AND GRASSLAND

To warn enemies away from their territory in the rain forest, howler monkeys make one of the loudest sounds in the animal kingdom. Every morning and evening, they howl in chorus, their throats swelling up like balloons. This sound can be heard up to 5 miles away!

Howler monkey

Woolly opossum

The woolly opossum is perfectly designed for a life high up in the rain forest trees. Its hands and feet are adapted for gripping on to tree branches as it searches for food. While feeding, it can hang by its long tail to reach fruits or flower nectar. Opossums are marsupials—mammals whose young develop inside pouches on their mothers' stomachs. Most species of marsupial live in Australasia (see page 26).

Related to raccoons, kinkajous are small mammals with long bodies and long tails. Like some monkeys, they use their tail as an extra limb for grasping on to tree branches. They feed only on fruit and other sweet food, probing flowers with their long tongues to reach the nectar.

Kinkajou

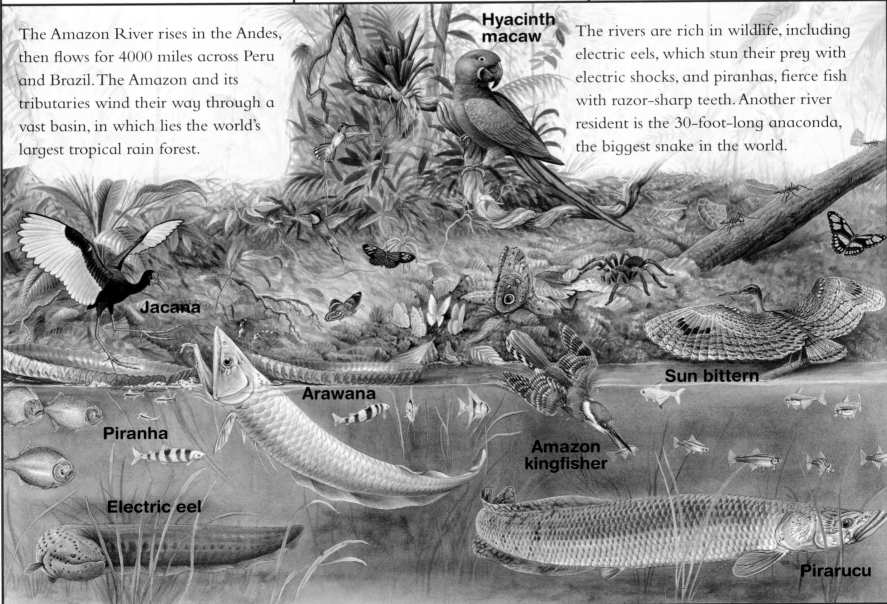

The Amazon River rises in the Andes, then flows for 4000 miles across Peru and Brazil. The Amazon and its tributaries wind their way through a vast basin, in which lies the world's largest tropical rain forest.

The rivers are rich in wildlife, including electric eels, which stun their prey with electric shocks, and piranhas, fierce fish with razor-sharp teeth. Another river resident is the 30-foot-long anaconda, the biggest snake in the world.

Hyacinth macaw

Jacana

Sun bittern

Arawana

Piranha

Amazon kingfisher

Electric eel

Pirarucu

The Amazon rain forest is incredibly rich in wildlife—a single rain forest tree may be home to 1500 species of insect alone. About two-thirds of all rain forest animals live high up in the canopy, the mass of leaves and branches that forms an almost continuous "roof" over the forest. They include monkeys, frogs, butterflies, and birds such as the toucan and scarlet macaw. Toucans use their long bills to pick fruit from branches. Macaws feed on nuts, seeds, and fruits, using their powerful tongues and beaks.

Morpho butterfly

Toucan

Scarlet macaw

Tapir

Anaconda

Jaguar

Jaguars roam the gloomy forest floor, hunting their prey of tapir, deer, birds, and rodents. They are also excellent swimmers and agile climbers.

Despite their small size, leaf-cutter or parasol ants are immensely strong. They can lift about 50 times their own weight in leaves. The ants cut up the leaves and carry them back across the forest floor to their underground nest. There, they chew up the pieces, and mix them with droppings and saliva to make a type of compost heap. On this, they cultivate fungus to eat. Another resident of the forest floor, the bird-eating spider, is the world's largest spider. Although it is large enough to prey on small birds, this is rare. It usually eats insects and small reptiles.

Hummingbird

Bush cricket

Leafcutter ants

Bird-eating spider

Three-toed sloth

The three-toed sloth spends most of its life hanging upside down from the rain forest trees. A leaf-eater, it moves extremely slowly, sometimes only a few feet a day. The sloth grips on to a branch with its long, hooked claws. Even its fur grows down from its stomach towards its back so that the rain runs off it. Microscopic green plants, called algae, grow on the sloth's fur.

AMAZON RAIN FOREST

AFRICA

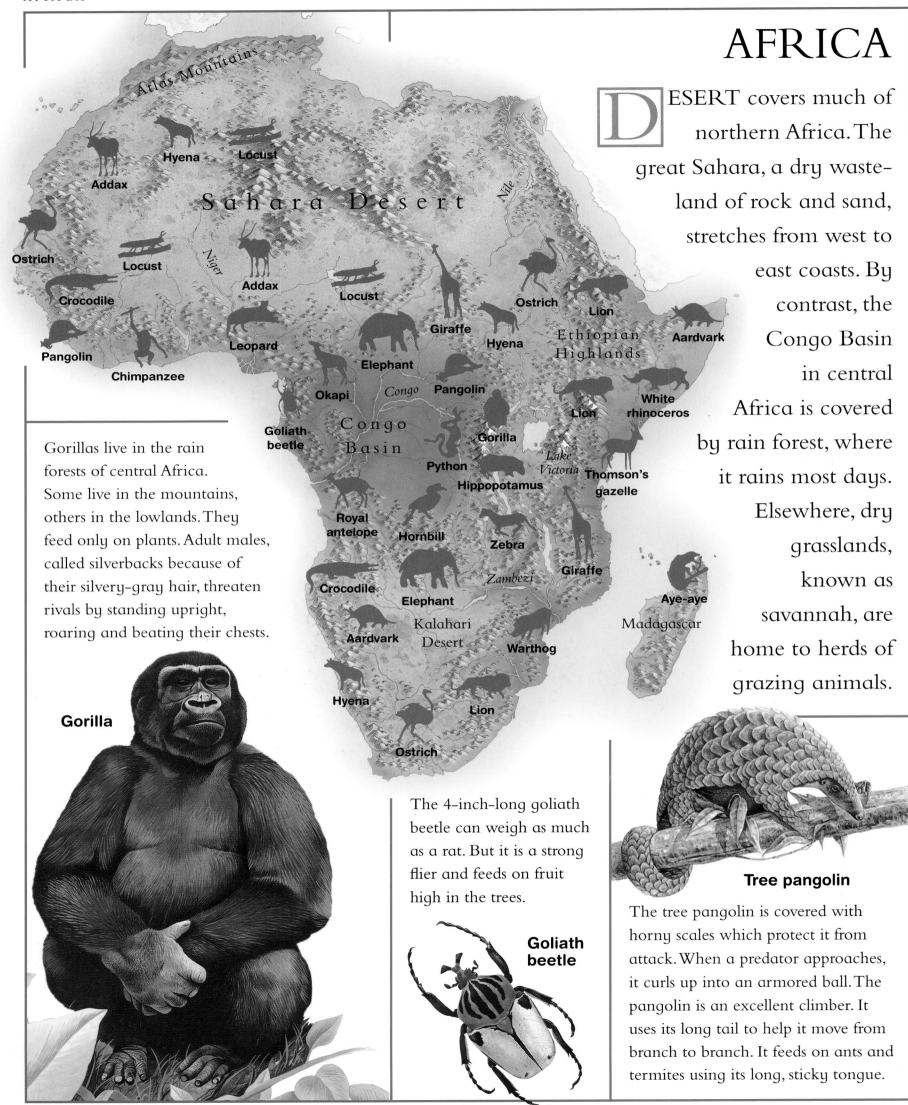

DESERT covers much of northern Africa. The great Sahara, a dry wasteland of rock and sand, stretches from west to east coasts. By contrast, the Congo Basin in central Africa is covered by rain forest, where it rains most days. Elsewhere, dry grasslands, known as savannah, are home to herds of grazing animals.

Gorillas live in the rain forests of central Africa. Some live in the mountains, others in the lowlands. They feed only on plants. Adult males, called silverbacks because of their silvery-gray hair, threaten rivals by standing upright, roaring and beating their chests.

Gorilla

The 4-inch-long goliath beetle can weigh as much as a rat. But it is a strong flier and feeds on fruit high in the trees.

Goliath beetle

Tree pangolin

The tree pangolin is covered with horny scales which protect it from attack. When a predator approaches, it curls up into an armored ball. The pangolin is an excellent climber. It uses its long tail to help it move from branch to branch. It feeds on ants and termites using its long, sticky tongue.

This strange member of the lemur family is found only in the rain forests of northeastern Madagascar. Moving around the branches at night, it uses its batlike ears to listen for insect grubs. Its long, thin middle fingers will then scrape them out from under the bark of a tree. It also eats fruit and eggs. The aye-aye is now very rare, partly because of the loss of its habitat, but also because it has been hunted by local people, who think it brings them bad luck.

Leopard

Python

Aye-aye

Predators use the lower branches of rain forest trees as a place to hide before they attack. The tiny royal antelope, only 16 inches long, is preyed upon by large snakes and leopards. The python will wrap its long body around its prey, then squeeze it to death. The leopard will leap down on its victim from above, then drag the kill back up into the tree for safety.

Royal antelope

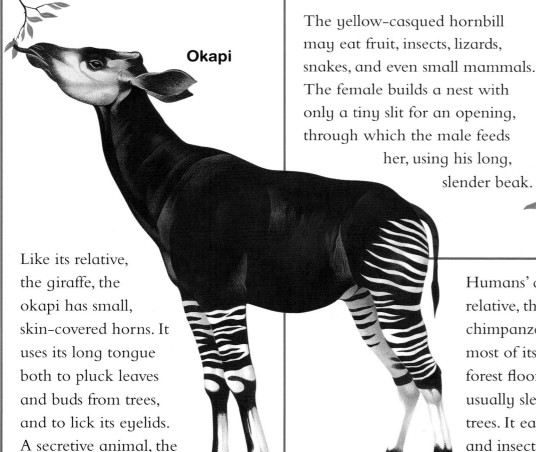

Okapi

Like its relative, the giraffe, the okapi has small, skin-covered horns. It uses its long tongue both to pluck leaves and buds from trees, and to lick its eyelids. A secretive animal, the okapi was discovered only 100 years ago.

The yellow-casqued hornbill may eat fruit, insects, lizards, snakes, and even small mammals. The female builds a nest with only a tiny slit for an opening, through which the male feeds her, using his long, slender beak.

Yellow-casqued hornbill

Humans' closest relative, the chimpanzee, spends most of its time on the forest floor although it usually sleeps in the trees. It eats fruit, eggs, and insects. Troops of chimps will also hunt monkeys for food.

Chimpanzee

RAIN FOREST

Addax

The addax is a large antelope that lives on the edges of the Sahara Desert. It has large, widely-spread hooves that allow it to walk easily on soft sand. Roaming in herds of up to 200 animals, the addax never drinks. It gets all the water it needs from the grasses it eats. It always knows exactly where to find vegetation that sprouts just after a downpour.

When the rains come to dry regions of northern Africa, desert locusts take to the air in vast swarms of up to 50 billion insects. Carried by the winds, they can eat an entire field of crops in a few minutes.

Desert locust

The ostrich, the world's largest bird, lives on Africa's dry grasslands. Too big to fly, it is the fastest creature on two legs. Its powerful legs and two-toed feet take it across the ground at speeds of up to 45 mph.

Ostrich

Ostriches mostly feed on plant shoots, leaves, flowers, and seeds. Females lay their eggs in a shallow pit dug in the sandy soil. Ostrich eggs are the largest laid by any bird—about 40 times the size of a hen's egg!

The savannah grasslands of Africa are areas dominated by grass, but there are also scattered bushes and trees. The climate is hot and there is a dry season followed by a rainy season. The savannah is home to many kinds of plant-eating animals *(opposite)*. They themselves are prey to some powerful carnivores, such as lions. Lionesses do most of the hunting, acting together to stalk and bring down zebra, antelope, and gazelle. The male lion, which heads a pride of up to three males and 15 females, along with their young, defends the pride's territory against other male lions.

Hyenas specialize in feeding on the kill of lions and other large carnivores. They often drive away other, smaller, predators. They use their powerful jaws to crush bones and extract the marrow.

Hyena

Warthog

Lion

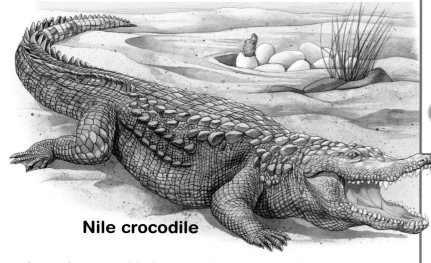

Nile crocodile

Aardvark

The aardvark is a secretive animal. It forages alone at night for food, using its keen senses of smell and hearing to seek out termites. It uses its claws to break open nests.

The Nile crocodile lives in the rivers and lakes of Africa—not just the Nile River. It preys on any animal, large or small, that dares to come to the water's edge to drink. The female lays her eggs in a pit near the water. She guards her eggs and the hatchlings very carefully.

Thomson's gazelles feed on short grass in the savannah of East Africa. They gather in large herds. When alarmed, they jump on all four legs. This is known as "pronking."

Thomson's gazelle

The vast areas of grass in the African savannah provide plentiful food for a wide range of grazing animals. They include zebra, which feed on the coarse tops, and gazelles, which eat the shoots close to the ground. The trees are also a food source: Giraffes eat leaves from the uppermost branches. Rhinoceroses browse on smaller shrubs and plants. Hippopotamuses spend most of their time in rivers and lakes. This keeps them cool in the hot African sunshine. In the evenings, the hippos emerge to feed on grass and fallen fruit.

White rhinoceros

Zebra

Hippopotamus

Giraffe

Elephant

GRASSLAND AND DESERT

Iceland

NORWEGIAN SEA

Brown bear

Brown bear

Burnet moth

Brown bear

Moose

Moose

The bright colors of the burnet moth are not simply for show. They indicate to hungry birds that the moth is poisonous and inedible.

DID YOU KNOW . . ?
The Mediterranean Sea in southern Europe is home to one of the world's rarest mammals. The monk seal once lived all around this region, but so much of its wild habitat has been lost that it now faces extinction.

Green woodpecker

British Isles

NORTH SEA

Badger

Moose

Fox

Fox

BALTIC SEA

Badger

Wild boar

Badger

Fox

North European Plain

Saiga

Volga

Badger

Hedgehog

Fox

Green woodpecker

Hedgehog

ATLANTIC OCEAN

Tawny owl

Badger

Fox

Cockchafer

Carpathians

Green woodpecker

Fox

Alps

Fox

Hedgehog

Wild boar

Wild boar

Wild boar

Brown bear

Cockchafer

Badger

BLACK SEA

Hedgehog

Wild boar

Brown bear

Wild boar

Tawny owl

MEDITERRANEAN SEA

Fox

ASIA

Wild boar

AFRICA

EUROPE

EUROPE has a very varied landscape which can be roughly divided into the cooler north and the warmer south. The far north is mostly blanketed with thick, coniferous forest. Here, winters are long and cold. The south of Europe, bordering the Mediterranean Sea, is much warmer and drier. Much of Europe was once covered with woods but many areas have been cleared for farming.

European badger

The European badger spends the day in its underground home, or sett. It only comes out at night to forage for its food of earthworms, beetles, and berries. A sett is a complex series of tunnels and chambers where generations of badgers may live for hundreds of years. Litters of badger cubs are born in the sett in spring.

Found all over Europe, red foxes will feed on almost anything, from mice and rabbits to birds and fruit. As their natural woodland habitat is reduced, many foxes have adapted to life in cities and towns. They come out at night to raid people's garbage cans for scraps of food, and may even make their "earths," or dens, in people's yards.

Red fox

The hooting sound of tawny owls may be heard in towns, cities, and woodlands right across Europe. The owl is perfectly equipped to hunt at night. It has superb hearing and can see well in the dark. In fact, a tawny owl's eyes can collect one hundred times more light than a pigeon's. Its wings have soft, fringed feathers which enable it to fly almost silently and swoop down unawares on its prey of voles, and mice. The owl carries them away in its sharp, curved talons.

Tawny owl

Wild boar

The ancestors of domestic hogs, wild boar roam through woodlands in many countries of mainland Europe. They are most active at nightfall, when they forage for food. Wild boar will eat almost anything, from fungi, wild bulbs, and nuts to snails, mice and young rabbits.

Green woodpecker

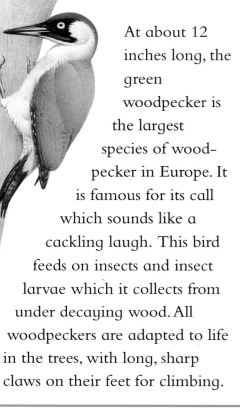

At about 12 inches long, the green woodpecker is the largest species of wood-pecker in Europe. It is famous for its call which sounds like a cackling laugh. This bird feeds on insects and insect larvae which it collects from under decaying wood. All woodpeckers are adapted to life in the trees, with long, sharp claws on their feet for climbing.

Cockchafer

The cockchafer, or may bug, is a common type of beetle which measures about 1 inch long. It can be seen flying about on warm evenings in early summer. As it flies, it spreads its feathery antennae into a fan. This helps it to detect the scent of food or a mate.

Hedgehogs are among the most familiar small mammals found in Europe. Easily identified by their thick, spiny coats, they can roll themselves into a tight, prickly ball if they are threatened. Hedgehogs eat a wide variety of insects but their main prey is earthworms. They will also scavenge on the bodies of dead animals and steal eggs and chicks from birds' nests.

Hedgehog

EUROPE

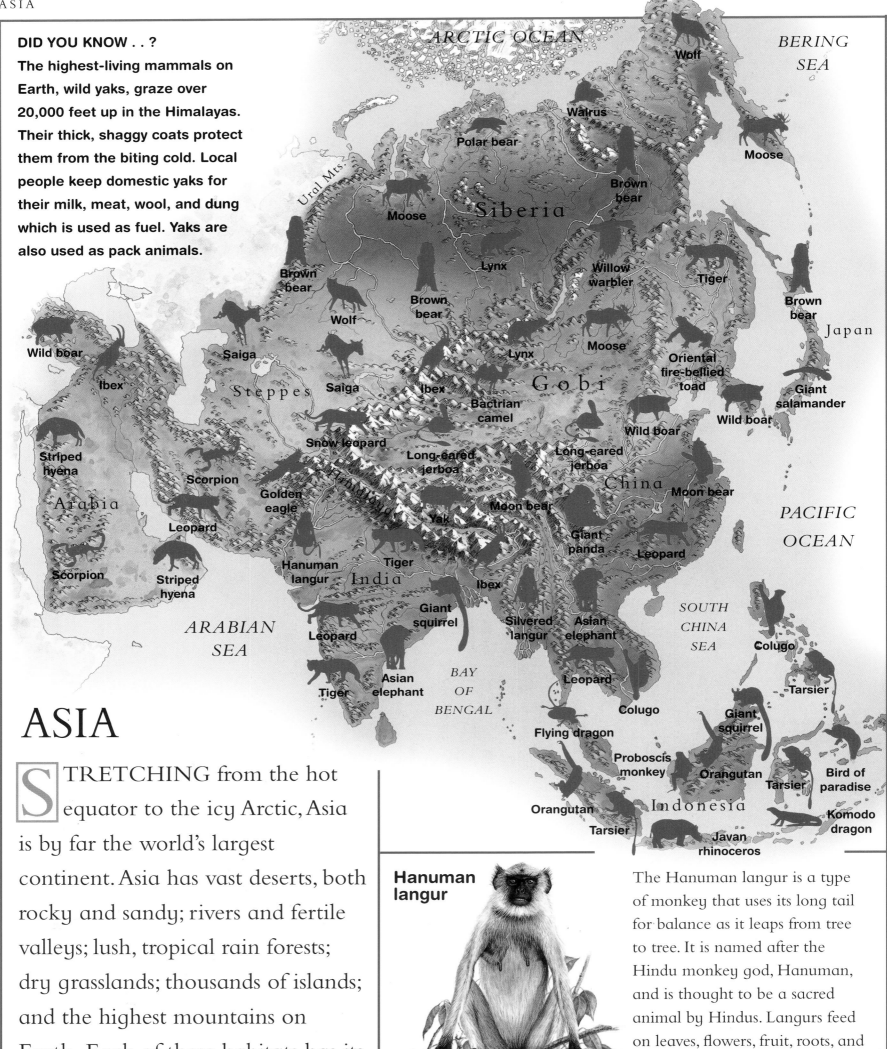

The highest-living mammals on Earth, wild yaks, graze over 20,000 feet up in the Himalayas. Their thick, shaggy coats protect them from the biting cold. Local people keep domestic yaks for their milk, meat, wool, and dung which is used as fuel. Yaks are also used as pack animals.

ARCTIC OCEAN

BERING SEA

Wolf

Walrus

Polar bear

Moose

Ural Mts.

Brown bear

Siberia

Moose

Brown bear

Tiger

Brown bear

Japan

Lynx

Willow warbler

Brown bear

Wolf

Wild boar

Ibex

Saiga

Lynx

Moose

Oriental fire-bellied toad

Steppes

Saiga

Ibex

Gobi

Giant salamander

Bactrian camel

Striped hyena

Scorpion

Snow leopard

Long-eared jerboa

Long-eared jerboa

Wild boar

Wild boar

China

Arabia

Golden eagle

Himalayas

Moon bear

Moon bear

PACIFIC OCEAN

Leopard

Yak

Giant panda

Scorpion

Striped hyena

Hanuman langur

Tiger

India

Ibex

Leopard

SOUTH CHINA SEA

ARABIAN SEA

Leopard

Giant squirrel

Silvered langur

Asian elephant

Colugo

Tiger

Asian elephant

BAY OF BENGAL

Leopard

Tarsier

Colugo

Giant squirrel

Flying dragon

Proboscis monkey

Bird of paradise

Orangutan

Tarsier

Orangutan

Indonesia

Komodo dragon

Tarsier

Javan rhinoceros

ASIA

STRETCHING from the hot equator to the icy Arctic, Asia is by far the world's largest continent. Asia has vast deserts, both rocky and sandy; rivers and fertile valleys; lush, tropical rain forests; dry grasslands; thousands of islands; and the highest mountains on Earth. Each of these habitats has its own communities of animals.

Hanuman langur

The Hanuman langur is a type of monkey that uses its long tail for balance as it leaps from tree to tree. It is named after the Hindu monkey god, Hanuman, and is thought to be a sacred animal by Hindus. Langurs feed on leaves, flowers, fruit, roots, and fungi. They also regularly raid farmers' fields for food.

Giant panda

Giant pandas live in the mountain forests of south-west China. They mostly eat bamboo shoots and may spend up to 16 hours a day feeding. Once widespread in China, these shy animals are now very rare. As people have taken over more of the bamboo forest for farmland, the giant pandas have lost vital sources of their food.

Japanese giant salamander

The Japanese giant salamander is the world's largest amphibian, growing up to 5 feet in length, including its long tail. It lives in cool mountain creeks and rivers where the water supports the weight of its body. In the water, the giant salamander takes in oxygen through the warty folds of skin that run along its sides. It also has lungs for breathing air when it comes to the surface. This strange-looking animal feeds on fish, worms and shellfish which it sucks up with its large, gaping mouth.

The mighty Himalayas are an enormous chain of mountains that stretch for some 1,600 miles right across Kashmir, northern India, Nepal, Bhutan, and Tibet. They are the highest mountains on Earth, with nine out of 10 of the world's highest peaks, including the highest of all, Mount Everest. The Himalayas provide a wide variety of habitats for animals, depending on how high you go.

In the foothills are thick forests where bears, pikas, and gorals roam. Higher up, above the treeline, it is bitterly cold and windy. Animals that live here, such as the Himalayan ibex, together with its powerful predator, the snow leopard, head downhill to the warmer, lower slopes in winter. Only a few insects can survive on the highest slopes where it is cold and icy all year round. These hardy creatures feed on tiny grains of pollen blown up by the wind.

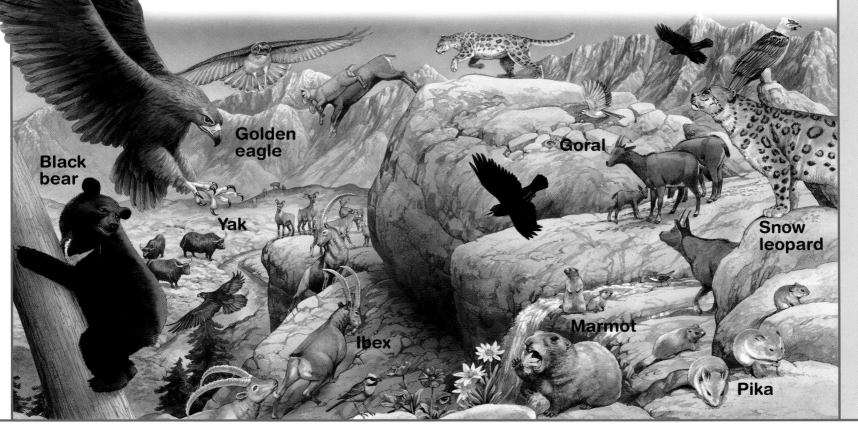

Golden eagle

Black bear

Yak

Goral

Snow leopard

Ibex

Marmot

Pika

Brown bear

Willow warblers are small birds with fine, pointed beaks for catching their prey of insects. In summer, the warblers nest in Siberia in northern Asia. But in winter, they travel thousands of miles to reach the warmer climate of Africa in search of food.

Willow warbler

The moose, or elk, lives in the northern forests of Siberia, northern Europe and North America. The world's largest deer, a male moose stands up to 6.5 feet tall and can weigh as much as half a ton. Moose browse on plants and may eat more than 20,000 leaves a day.

Moose

The brown bear of the northern Asian forests survives the long cold winter months when food is scarce by hibernating in its den. It lives on stores of body fat which it builds up in the fall when there is plenty of food about. The bear's den may be in a hollow tree or in a cave. It is here that female bears give birth to their cubs in February or March. The cubs stay in the den until May or June. They may remain close to their mother until they are about 4 years old.

Floating among a pond's water weeds, an oriental fire-bellied toad is well camouflaged by the green skin on its back. But if attacked, it will display the bright, fire-colored belly that gives it its name. This warns the toad's enemies that it is highly poisonous to eat.

Siberian tiger

Oriental fire-bellied toad

At up to 10 feet long, the Siberian tiger is the largest of the big cats. It is also one of the rarest, with only about 400 tigers left in the wild. Thick fur and belly fat keep it warm in the Siberian cold.

Bactrian camel

Long-eared jerboa

Long and powerful back legs allow the long-eared jerboa to leap over the desert ground at high speed. Its large ears help it to listen for danger when it ventures out of its burrow at night to find seeds, insects, and plant scraps to eat.

Most two-humped Bactrian camels are domesticated, but some still live wild in the Central Asian deserts. Camels are ideal desert animals. They store fat in their humps for food, can drink around 30 gallons of water at a time and go days without drinking. They have broad, flat feet for walking over sand, and close their nostrils to keep out sand. In winter they grow long, shaggy fur and in summer they shed it to keep cool.

Striped hyena

In the desert, scorpions spend most of the day hiding under rocks. They only come out at dusk or dawn. Scorpions use the poisonous stingers at the ends of their tails to stun large prey and in self-defense.

Scorpion

Striped hyenas are master scavengers. They have powerful jaws for dealing with the parts of a kill, such as bones and hooves, that other animals leave behind. They also feed on fruit and vegetation which provide an important source of water in the dry grasslands.

The saiga antelope lives on the vast steppe, or grassland, which stretches across the central plains of Asia. Its bulging nose makes it easy to recognize. Its nose is thought to help filter out sand and dust in the dry summer, and to warm the cold air it breathes in during the winter months.

Saiga

FOREST, GRASSLAND, AND DESERT

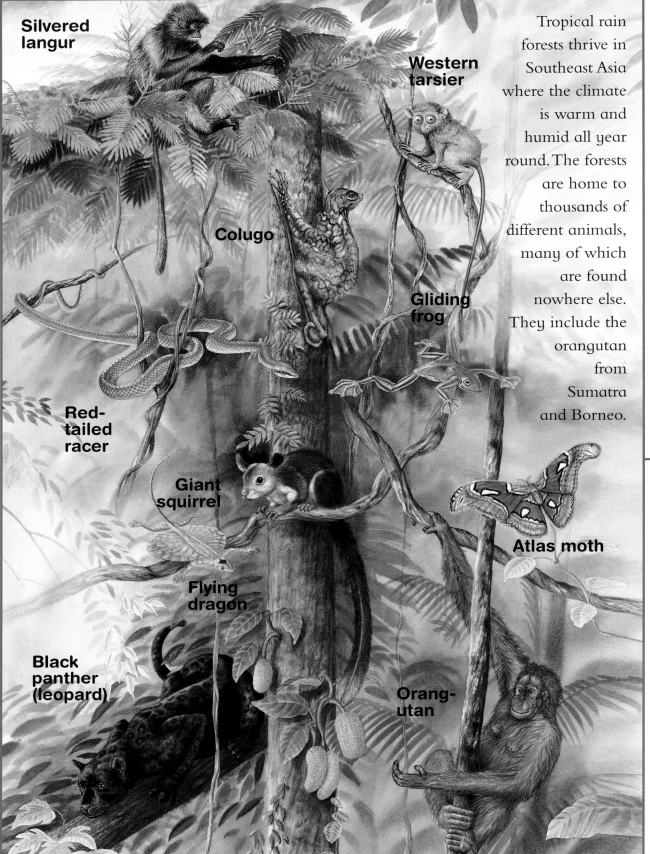

Silvered langur

Western tarsier

Colugo

Gliding frog

Red-tailed racer

Giant squirrel

Atlas moth

Flying dragon

Black panther (leopard)

Orang-utan

Tropical rain forests thrive in Southeast Asia where the climate is warm and humid all year round. The forests are home to thousands of different animals, many of which are found nowhere else. They include the orangutan from Sumatra and Borneo.

The male proboscis monkey has a very large, trunklike nose which hangs down over his mouth. It seems to be used as a loudspeaker for the male's honking calls that warn others of danger.

Proboscis monkey

Male birds of paradise are famous for their striking plumage which they use to attract a mate. They perform elaborate displays in the trees to show off their spectacular feathers. In contrast, females have dull brown coloring.

Bird of paradise

With its massive 10-foot-long body, the Komodo dragon is the largest lizard in the world. It lives only on Komodo and a few other islands in Indonesia. This giant reptile has long, jagged teeth for grabbing its prey of wild hogs, deer, and goats. Then it shakes its victims to death. The dragon can dislocate its lower jaws to enable it to swallow its prey whole.

Komodo dragon

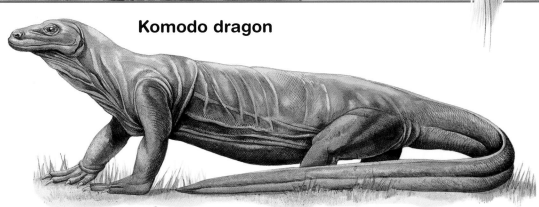

Tiger

Tigers are solitary hunters. They "stalk and ambush" their prey of deer, wild hogs, and other mammals. They will also feed on carcasses. Tigers mainly hunt in the twilight when their striped coats help to hide them in the dappled light of the forest floor. Once widespread across Asia, habitat loss and hunting have pushed tigers to the brink of extinction.

With a wingspan of over 11 inches, the Queen Alexandra bird-wing is the world's biggest butterfly. It spends much of its time high up in the rain forest trees.

Queen Alexandra's birdwing

Although Asian and African elephants look similar, there are several differences between the two. Asian elephants are smaller, with smaller ears and shorter tusks than African elephants. They are also easier to tame and are still used in many parts of South Asia for carrying people and heavy loads, such as lumber. These sociable animals live in small family groups, led by an elderly female. Males tend to live separately.

Asian elephant

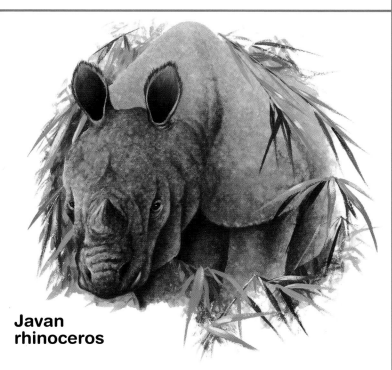

Javan rhinoceros

The Javan rhinoceros is the rarest of all the species of rhinoceros. Fewer than just 60 animals still survive in the rain forests of Indonesia and Vietnam. Threats to the rhinos' survival include habitat loss and hunting for their horns which are ground down and used in Chinese medicine. Poachers are paid large sums of money to find and kill rhinos for their horns.

SOUTHEAST ASIAN RAIN FOREST

INDIAN
OCEAN

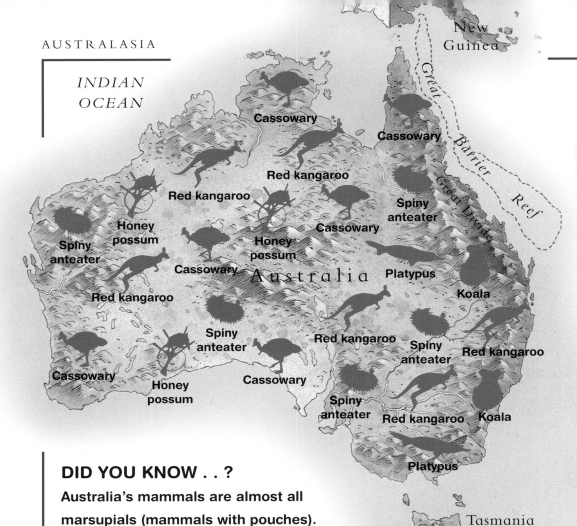

New
Guinea

Cassowary

Cassowary

Red kangaroo

Red kangaroo

Spiny
anteater

Honey
possum

Cassowary

Spiny
anteater

Honey
possum

Cassowary

Australia

Platypus

Koala

Red kangaroo

Spiny
anteater

Red kangaroo

Spiny
anteater

Cassowary

Honey
possum

Cassowary

Spiny
anteater

Red kangaroo

Koala

Platypus

Tasmania

Platypus

AUSTRALASIA

AUSTRALASIA is made up of the island continent of Australia, together with New Zealand and other nearby islands. Inland, most of Australia is empty desert. New Zealand has a warm, rainy climate. Australasia is home to some of the world's most unusual animals.

Giant weta

Kiwi

New
Zealand

Tuatara

Kiwi

DID YOU KNOW . . ?

Australia's mammals are almost all marsupials (mammals with pouches). Australia has over 150 species of marsupials. Outside Australia, marsupials are only found in South America, with one species in North America.

Duck-billed platypus

The duck-billed platypus lives in rivers, lakes, and creeks, and is well adapted to life in the water. It has webbed feet and a ducklike bill which it uses to probe for food in the mud. The platypus and spiny anteater, or echidna, are very unusual mammals. Instead of giving birth to live young, as most mammals do, they reproduce by laying eggs.

Spiny anteater

The biggest kind of marsupial, the red kangaroo stands more than 6 feet tall. It uses its 3-foot-long tails for balance as it bounds across the ground. A large male can cover more than 30 feet in a single leap. Like all marsupials, female red kangaroos have pouches which they use as nurseries for their young. A new-born kangaroo is blind, helpless and only about 5 inches long. It crawls up its mother's fur into her pouch where it attaches itself to one of her teats. It stays there for about 6 months, drinking milk and growing. At 28 weeks old, it makes its first journey outside the pouch but quickly hops back in if danger threatens. It leaves the pouch for good when it is about 9 months old.

Red kangaroo

Young in mother's pouch

Koala

Excellent climbers, koalas grip tree trunks and branches with their sharp claws and rarely come down to the ground. They feed almost entirely on eucalyptus trees and eat so many leaves each day that they actually smell of eucalyptus! But they are very fussy eaters. Of the 350 species of eucalyptus, koalas will only eat 20.

Cassowaries are large birds that live in the rain forests of New Guinea and Australia. They are related to emus and ostriches. Unable to fly, they can move speedily through the undergrowth on their long legs. They probably use the bony growths on their heads to turn over leaf litter on the ground to find their food of fruit, insects, snails, and fungi.

Cassowary

Giant weta

Giant wetas are large, stoutly built crickets found only on a few small islands off New Zealand. They have long back legs, bristling with spines, which they wave at their enemies to warn them to stay away. Wetas are nocturnal, coming out at night to feed on plants and fungi.

Tuatara

New Zealand has been cut off from the rest of the world for the last 80 million years. Many of its animals are not found anywhere else. Among the most famous are tuataras and kiwis. Tuataras belong to an ancient group of reptiles that survives from the time of the dinosaurs.

The kiwi is a shy, flightless bird, covered in long, shaggy brown feathers. It hunts for its food of insects and worms at night, listening for them with its sharp ears and sniffing them out with the nostrils at the tip of its long bill.

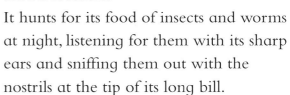
Kiwi

The honey possum from Western Australia is about the size of a mouse. It uses its pointed snout to probe into flowers for nectar and pollen. Its long, thin tongue is covered in bristles, with a tip like a fine brush. As the possum feeds, pollen and nectar stick to its tongue. Despite its name, the honey possum's diet does not include any honey.

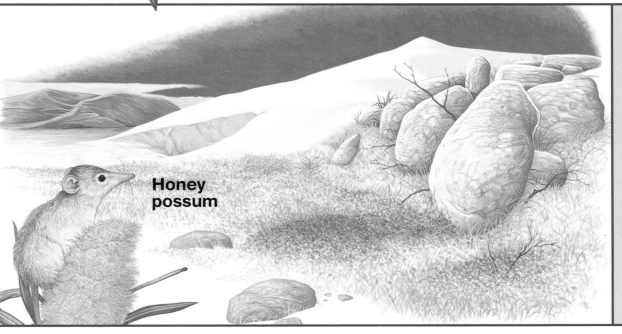
Honey possum

AUSTRALASIA

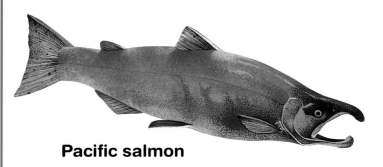

Pacific salmon

Every year, enormous numbers of salmon swim thousands of miles across the Pacific Ocean to rivers where they lay their eggs. They use their amazing memory and sense of smell to return to the same rivers in which they themselves hatched.

Gray whales spend the summer months feeding on shrimp and shellfish in the Arctic Ocean. Then they swim south along the Pacific coasts to breed in warm, shallow, sub-tropical waters

Gray whale

of East Asia and Mexico. They head north again in spring, completing a round trip of some 12,000 miles, the furthest of any mammal. As a result of years of hunting, gray whales are now endangered.

Sea otters live among the beds of giant kelp seaweed in the North Pacific. At night, they wrap strands of kelp around their bodies to stop them from drifting away with the currents as they sleep. By day, the otters dive for sea urchins, crabs, and shellfish to eat. Then they come to the surface and float on their backs. Using their bellies as tables, they smash the hard shells open with large rocks to reach the soft flesh inside.

Californian sea otter

Blue-footed booby

Blue-footed boobies are large seabirds, related to gannets. They nest on the steep cliff-faces of the Galapagos Islands, off the west coast of South America. They dive into the sea from the air to catch fish underwater. Their tapered bodies cut easily through the water. Their bills are long and sharply pointed, with serrated edges for gripping on to fish. Both male and female boobies have bright blue feet. Males display their feet during courtship to help them attract a mate.

Also known as "sea cows," manatees spend much of their time grazing on underwater plants and grasses. They live in shallow water along warm coasts. Despite their lumbering appearance, manatees are superb swimmers, capable of speeds of up to 15 mph. They wag their large, paddle-shaped tails up and down to propel their bodies through the water.

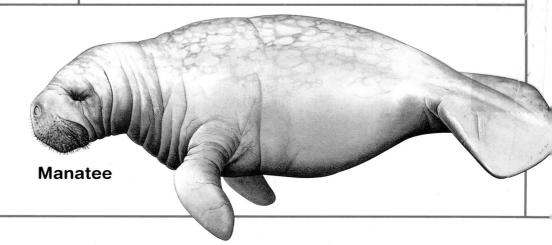

Manatee

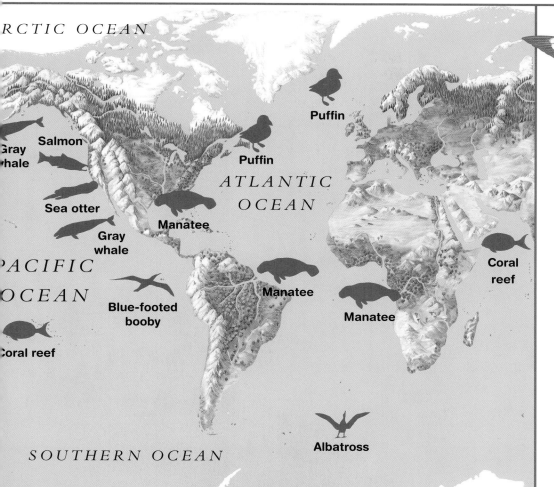

ARCTIC OCEAN

Gray whale

Salmon

Puffin

Puffin

ATLANTIC OCEAN

Sea otter

Manatee

Gray whale

PACIFIC OCEAN

Blue-footed booby

Manatee

Manatee

Coral reef

Coral reef

SOUTHERN OCEAN

Albatross

Wandering albatross

About 300 species of birds live on or near the ocean, feeding on fish and other marine life. The giant wandering albatross (seen above in its courtship ritual) glides and soars across the Southern Ocean. Its 10-foot wingspan is the largest of any bird. The puffin of the North Atlantic and Arctic flies strong and fast. It carries its catch in its colorful bill.

Puffin

Turtles are some of the many animals that live near coral reefs. At breeding time, females lay their eggs in nests dug in the sand on coral island beaches. Baby turtle hatchlings face a dangerous journey back to the sea. Many are eaten by gulls and crabs.

After dark, reef sharks prowl the reef edges on the look-out for food. These feared predators can sense the movements of injured fish and swiftly move in for the kill.

THE OCEANS

THE OCEANS form the largest habitat. Most animals live in the sunlit waters close to the surface.

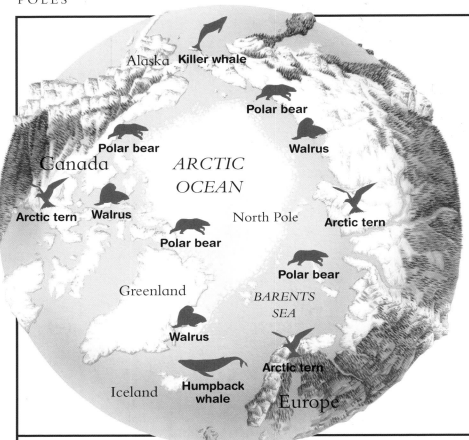

Alaska **Killer whale**

Polar bear

Polar bear **Walrus**

Canada ARCTIC OCEAN

Arctic tern **Walrus** North Pole **Arctic tern**

Polar bear

Polar bear

Greenland BARENTS SEA

Walrus

Iceland **Humpback whale** **Arctic tern** Europe

THE ARCTIC

THE NORTH POLE is situated in the Arctic Ocean. For most of the year, the ocean is covered by a thick layer of floating ice. Around its edges are pieces of broken ice, called pack ice.

Most Arctic life is found in and around the ocean. Tiny plants, called plankton, become plentiful in summer. They provide food for tiny animals, which are in turn eaten by fish, seals, birds, and whales.

Polar bears live on the ice floes and frozen shores of the Arctic Ocean. They feed on seals by using their keen sense of smell to find their dens, or waiting for them to surface at breathing holes in the ice. They also hunt fish, seabirds, hares, caribou and musk oxen. Polar bears can travel long distances each day in search of prey. Sometimes they must swim for many hours in the icy waters.

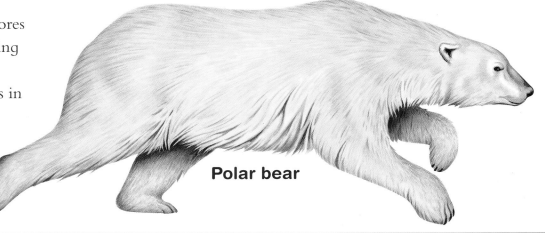

Polar bear

Walrus

Walruses huddle together in their hundreds on the Arctic ice. If there is no room on the ground, they will happily lie on top of one another! They feed on shell-fish, shrimps, and crabs dug up from the sea bed with their snouts. Their tusks are used both to prize shellfish off rocks and haul their own bodies out of the water.

Killer whale

At up to 33 feet long, the killer whale is the largest of the dolphin family. It can be found in all oceans, but is commonest in polar waters. Killer whales live and hunt together in groups, called pods. They catch fish by herding shoals into shallow water where they can be caught more easily. Killers also prey on seals, sea lions, seabirds, other dolphins, and even large whales.

The emperor penguin is the largest kind of penguin. A graceful swimmer, it gets about on the ice by sliding on its belly! After laying her single egg, the female leaves her male partner to look after the egg. He carries it on his feet where it is protected by a flap of skin. All the males huddle together for warmth. When the chick hatches out, it remains protected on his feet.

Emperor penguin

Arctic tern

The Arctic tern spends the summer months in the Arctic, raising its young. Then it flies all the way to Antarctica, a distance of some 8000 miles, where it spends a second summer fishing off the coast. It then returns north. This bird makes the longest migration journey of any animal. Over the course of its life it may fly more than 600,000 miles.

Every summer, humpback whales migrate from tropical waters to feed in Antarctic waters. They are known for their "singing"— chirping and yupping sounds that travel for hundreds of miles. Humpbacks are also acrobats. They can leap backwards out of the water.

Humpback whale

DID YOU KNOW . . ?

Many polar mammals have thick fur coats. Others have layers of fat, called blubber, under their skins to keep them warm. Birds' feathers do a similar job. The penguin's short, glossy feathers form a dense mat that keeps the water out and the warmth in.

ANTARCTICA

THE CONTINENT of Antarctica is a mountainous land almost completely covered by a permanent ice cap. Pack ice and icebergs float in the surrounding ocean waters. Plankton also provides food for Antarctic animals. Giant whales feed on krill, small shrimplike animals.

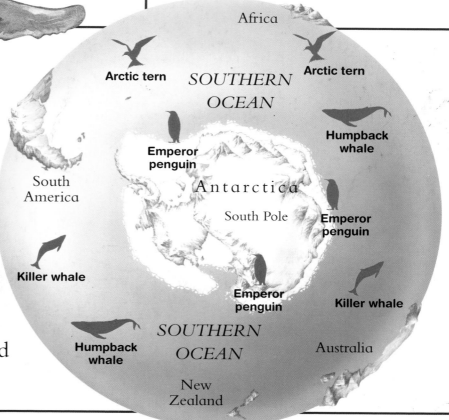

Africa

Arctic tern

SOUTHERN OCEAN

Arctic tern

Humpback whale

Emperor penguin

South America

Antarctica

South Pole

Emperor penguin

Killer whale

Emperor penguin

Killer whale

SOUTHERN OCEAN

Humpback whale

Australia

New Zealand

INDEX